Cake Decorating

Wedding Designs

Lorraine Sorby-Howlett
&
Marian Jones

MEREHURST PRESS

CONTENTS

MY ROSE	5
ON THIS DAY	6
FALLING BLOSSOMS	8
DREAMS COME TRUE	11
CRYSTAL DELIGHT	13
ORCHID FANTASY	15
LEMON ELEGANCE	16
CANDLELIGHT	17
YOUR DREAM	18
LOVE HEARTS	19
SO BEAUTIFUL	20
SWEET FRANGIPANI	21
SWEET BOUQUET	22
TROPICAL JEWEL	23
SUNNY DAY	24
DIAMONDS ARE FOREVER	26
RED VELVET	28
L'AMOUR	29
TRAILING ROSES	30
FLEUR	31
MELODY OF LOVE	32
APRICOT LACE	33
SUMMER LACE	34
PROMISE ME	35
DAINTY BELLS	36
LUCKY IN LOVE	37
SWEET AND PRETTY	38
JOY	39
ALL OUR DREAMS	40
FIRST LOVE	42
WEDDING BELLS	43
AUTUMN HAZE	44
PINK PEARL	45
PINK ELEGANCE	46
WISHING	47
APRIL LOVE	48
CHARMING CASCADE	49
BLUE LACE	50
JUST PERFECT	51
BOUQUET OF HAPPINESS	52
SO IN LOVE	53
TODAY, TOMORROW, ALWAYS	54
CINDERELLA	57
ROMANCE	58
BE MY LOVE	59
FANTASIA	60
RHAPSODY IN PINK	61
ANGEL ORCHIDS	62
MODERN BRIDE	63

Published 1992 Merehurst Limited
Reprinted 1993, 1994
Ferry House
51/57 Lacy Road
Putney
London
SW15 1PR

ISBN 1-85391-113-5

FOREWORD

What a pleasure and a privilege it is to be asked to write a foreword to this book.

For many years in Australia there was a dearth of cake decorating books to help brides and cake decorators alike.

Then the boom started and within a short period of time books, written by Australian cake decorators, came onto the market. They were many and varied; books for beginners, advanced decorators and teachers. How grateful we have been for them all.

Cake decorating is an art which Australian women have lifted to a very high standard in the eyes of the world, but it is also a business, and in the business world we have supply and demand!

In the business of wedding cakes the demand can be for cakes of the highest quality, put together with loving care, with money no object. These cakes can be supplied by so many of our highly qualified cake decorators, who prefer to take their time to skilfully provide this service.

But there is also a great demand, especially in large cities, for simple, less expensive cakes, which a bride can still expect to look pretty, and to match in with the theme of her wedding.

So many of our top cake decorators supply this type of wedding cake and they do it skilfully and successfully, still personally designing simple, individual cakes for each bride.

I was delighted to hear that Lorraine and Marian had decided to put some of their cakes and imaginative ideas together and publish them in what I consider to be a new and unusual book.

Most of the cakes are simple, but attractive, and some quite different! It will therefore appeal to those already accomplished in the art of cake decorating. It should also appeal to brides who want the assurance that the cake will look exactly as it does in the book, and this book has been presented in such a way that any cake decorator using it can give that assurance with confidence.

Good luck, Lorraine and Marian. I hope that all your hard work is rewarded with a most successful publication.

Shirley Lennox
Canberra

MY ROSE

The simplicity of the single rose gives a magic touch to this cake. The delicate heart edging adds the promise of true love.

SPECIAL NOTE:
Frill heart cutters are used for the edging.

You will need:

To Bake	1 large scalloped oval 1 small scalloped oval
Boards	base board 50 mm (2 inch) larger all round than large cake top board same size as cake
Flowers	1 large formal rose 3 leaves
Ribbons	1 double loop with long tails

ON THIS DAY

A romantic design for that special day. The flooded bride and groom on the top tier are complimented by the dainty lace finish and simple floral arrangement of kurume azaleas and rosebuds.

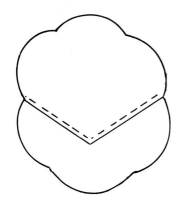

You will need:

To Bake	1 large blossom shaped cake, cut to achieve the fan shape
	1 small blossom shaped cake, cut to achieve the fan shape
Boards	base board 50 mm (2 inch) larger than the cut cake shape
	top board 25 mm (1 inch) larger than the cut cake shape
Flowers	8 kurume azaleas
	10 rose buds
	18 sprays of sweet rocket flowers
Ribbons	8 bunches of small loops
	1 tiny bunch for the bride's bouquet

Cutting line for both cakes

The superb detail of the bridal party is shown here. The lace on the dresses is shaded.

7

FALLING BLOSSOMS

This delightful cake will appeal to the modern bride. The top tier is set off-centre with spring flowers cascading from a hand-moulded bell on the top tier to the apron of the bottom tier, then falling delicately onto the board.

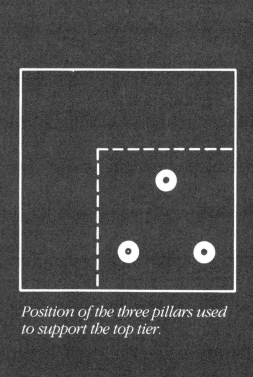

Position of the three pillars used to support the top tier.

You will need:

To Bake	1 – 25 cm (10 inch) square cake
	1 – 15 cm (6 inch) square cake
Boards	1 – 33 cm (13 inch) square
	1 – 20 cm (8 inch) square
Flowers	72 spring blossoms
	30 jasmine
	10 sprays of white lilac
	22 leaves
Ribbons	1 large florist bow for behind the bell
	11 small bunches of 2 mm (1/16 inch) white satin ribbon
Bell	75 mm (3 inch) back-blushed and embroidered and finished with lace pieces

SPECIAL NOTE:

Once again note that the boards are flooded with royal icing and finished with narrow silver edging. The flowers are coloured by the spray painting method. Special 38 mm (1½ inch) pillars were used to lower the top tier to achieve the cascading effect.

Position of hand-moulded bell with the delicate edging, floral bow and spray painted cascade.

9

DREAMS COME TRUE

This cake features a wedding bell on the top tier spilling beautiful flowers which compliment the church embroidery which is the focal point of each tier.

Details of church embroidery.

Detail of hand-moulded bell with ribbon tufts among the delicately painted flowers.

You will need:

To Bake	3 hexagonal cakes
Boards (flooded)	large board allow 38 mm (1½ inch) all round tin size middle board allow 32 mm (1¼ inch) top board allow 25 mm (1 inch)
Flowers	108 mountain primula – delicately spray painted in apricot 50 pulled jasmine – no buds 46 tiny leaves
Ribbons	1 large florist bow behind the bell 16 looped 2 mm (1/16 inch) ribbon tufts

SPECIAL NOTE:

You will need to mould a 75 mm (3 inch) bell and delicately blush colour on the rim of the bell shading towards the back. (This method is called back blushing). Embroider the bell before attaching to the cake. Arrange the flowers and florist bow and finish off with lace pieces around rim of the bell.

Variation using floral embroidery.

The acrylic stand can be seen more clearly here without the crystal ornament and floral display.

CRYSTAL DELIGHT

The simple and elegant styling of this different arrangement featuring acrylic stand and crystal ornament filled with flowers, makes this a most delightful cake. Crystal ornaments are becoming very fashionable as the bride may keep them as a reminder of her special day.

You will need:

To Bake	2 medium octagonal cakes
	1 small bell
Boards	2 octagonal 25 mm (1 inch) larger all round than the tin
Flowers	50 Cecil Brunner roses
	10 rosebuds
	15 sprays field flowers
	16 mock orange blossom
	50 tiny filler flowers
	30 wired rose leaves
Ribbon	30 bunches of medium ribbon loops with tails

Variation using only two tiers but enhanced with a latticed stand.

ORCHID FANTASY

A dynamic, different three tier scalloped oval cake. Large Zygo orchids, fairy bells and tiny apple berry flowers combine with crystal pillars to achieve the fantasy effect.

You will need:

To Bake	3 scalloped oval cakes
Boards	Large base board 50 mm (2 inch) larger than the tin Middle board the same size as the tin used Top board 25 mm (1 inch) larger than the tin
Flowers	6 Zygo orchids 38 fairy bells 27 sprays apple berry 17 wired leaves
Ribbons	3 mm (⅛ inch) around the base as well as in 20 bunches of ribbon loops

SPECIAL NOTE:

Floral top is formed onto heavy gauge wire into the perspex base and placed in position when completed, see close-up right.

Detail of large Zygo orchid display using ribbon loops and fairy bells.

LEMON ELEGANCE

Frangipanis, morning glory roses, rosebuds, apple blossom and small leaves compliment the wedding scroll and rings on this single tier cake. The flooded board was used to compliment the pretty frilled edge.

You will need:

To Bake	1 – 23 cm (9 inch) square cake
Board (flooded)	30 cm (12 inch) with narrow gold foil edging
Flowers	4 frangipanis 3 medium morning glory roses 6 small morning glory roses 6 rosebuds 9 leaves 8 apple blossoms and buds
Ribbons	4 loops of 2 mm (1/16 inch) white satin ribbon
Frill	15 mm (½ inch) frill was attached to the cake and finished with an embroidery of tiny dots scattered all over. A fine band of eggshell lemon ribbon was used to finish off the frilled flounce

Detail of frangipani spray with wedding scroll and rings.

CANDLELIGHT

Romantically interlocked hearts, tapers and the unusual dianthus flowers, set the mood for a candlelight wedding.

You will need:

To Bake	2 heart shaped cakes of the same size
Board	base board 50 mm (2 inch) larger than the joined cakes
Flowers	22 dianthus 8 rock jasmine 12 sprigs white fabiana
Ribbons	8 small bunches
Additional Decoration	3 tapers

The tiny flowers around the base of the tapers can be shaded to match the bridesmaids' dresses.

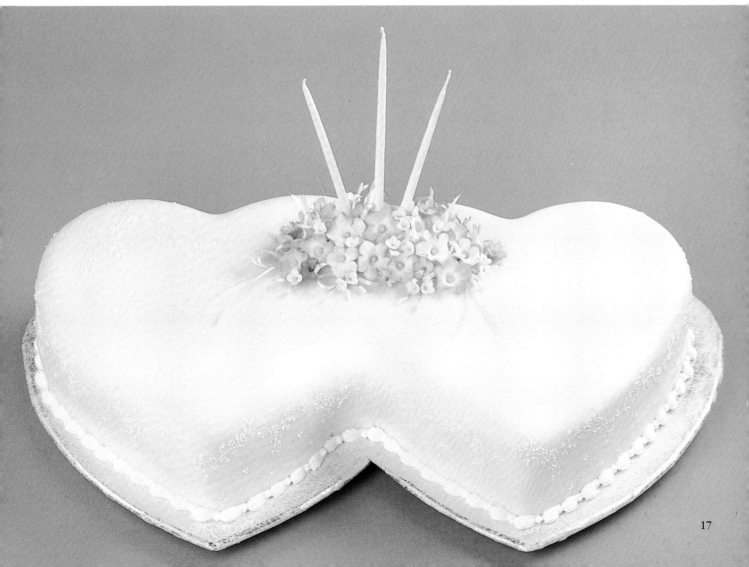

YOUR DREAM

The main attraction of this design is the lovely arrangement of briar roses and small sprays of flowers. The colour tonings can be varied to match the theme of the wedding.

You will need:

To Bake	3 hexagonal cakes
Boards	base board 50 mm (2 inch) larger all round than the cake middle and top boards 25 mm (1 inch) larger all round than the cakes
Flowers	31 briar roses 18 sprays of small flowers
Ribbons	10 bunches of loops with long tails 19 small bunches of loops

LOVE HEARTS

Formal roses, violets, jasmine and blossom make this heart shaped cake a pretty picture at any time of the year.

Variation on Love Hearts
Same as design used in Love Hearts but using octagonal cakes instead of hearts.

You will need:

To Bake	1 – 25 cm (10 inch) heart
	1 – 15 cm (6 inch) heart
Boards	base board 50 mm (2 inch) larger all round than large cake
	top board 25 mm (1 inch) larger all round than small cake
Flowers	9 formal roses
	16 bunches jasmine
	12 violets
	10 leaves
	10 blossom
Ribbons	12 bunches

19

SO BEAUTIFUL

An elegant design for the sophisticated bride. The embroidered pattern of the bridal gown is recreated in the fine piping and lacework of the cake.

You will need:

To Bake	1 large oval cake
	1 small oval cake
Boards	base board 50 mm (2 inch)
	larger all round than large cake
	top board 25 mm (1 inch larger
	all round than small cake
Flowers	5 large orchids
	21 sprays of honeysuckle
Ribbons	8 large bunches

SWEET FRANGIPANI

A simple, elegant cake featuring frangipani. An easy design with colours complimenting the flower arrangement.

You will need:

| To Bake | 1 – 25 cm (10 inch) round cake |
| | 1 – 15 cm (6 inch) round cake |

Boards   base board 75 mm (3 inch)
            larger all round than
            large cake
            top board 50 mm (2 inch)
            larger all round than
            small cake

Flowers   11 frangipani
              3 buds
              20 sprays Mexican orange
                  blossom
              15 violets

Ribbons   6 bunches

SPECIAL NOTE:
Lemon ribbon is used around
    the cake as well as in the
    sprays.

SWEET BOUQUET

A sweetly elegant cake in delicate colour shades. The dainty lace edge adds to the overall soft design. An easy cake for the beginner.

You will need:

To Bake   2 hexagonal cakes –
                1 large size
                1 small size

Boards	base board 10 cm (4 inch) larger all round than large cake top board 50 mm (2 inch) larger all round than small cake
Flowers	50 field flowers 30 beauty bush blossoms 20 leaves
Ribbons	25 small bunches

TROPICAL JEWEL

A truly delightful cake. The tropical colours in the orchids can be altered to suit the colour theme of your wedding party.

You will need:

To Bake	1–25 cm (10 inch) square cake
	1–20 cm (8 inch) square cake
	1–15 cm (6 inch) square cake
Boards	flooded boards need solid base
	base board 10 cm (4 inch) larger all round than large cake
	middle board 50 mm (2 inch) larger all round than medium cake
	small board 50 mm (2 inch) larger all round than small cake
Flowers	11 orchids
	30 blossoms
	25 jasmine
Ribbons	double rows around each tier
	12 medium bunches
	6 small bunches

SUNNY DAY

A beautiful arrangement for a two tier cake. The ivy leaf edge is echoed in the flower arrangement of azaleas and lilies-of-the-valley.

SPECIAL NOTE:
Lower edge of the cake is finished with ivy leaves in large and small sizes. You will need 50 large and 40 small to complete the design.

You will need:

To Bake	1 – 35 cm (14 inch) rectangle
	1 – 20 cm (8 inch) rectangle
Boards	base board 50 mm (2 inch) larger all round than large cake
	top board 25 mm (1 inch) larger all round than small cake
Flowers	10 silver slipper azaleas
	14 ivy leaves
	8 sprays of lily-of-the-valley
Ribbons	6 bunches of loops

Life-size detail of ivy leaves.

DIAMONDS ARE FOREVER

The unusual treatment of the board and lovely crystal birds set among the floral arrangement combine beautifully in this delightful design. Any colour combination would be suitable for this cake.

SPECIAL NOTE:
Top tier rests on a specially made diamond shaped perspex pillar.

You will need:

To Bake	1 large diamond shaped cake
	1 small diamond shaped cake
Boards	base board 50 mm (2 inch) larger all round than large cake
	top board 25 mm (1 inch) larger all round than small cake
Flowers	15 Java orchids
	18 sprays of tiny flowers and buds
Ribbons	15 small bunches of loops

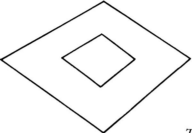

Top tier set at back of base tier.

The aqua crystal birds are surrounded by dainty primrose-coloured flowers.

RED VELVET

Delicate embroidery and lacework make this design a pretty picture. The touch of red on the edging emphasises the beautiful carnations in the floral arrangement.

You will need:

To Bake	1 – 25 cm (10 inch) round cake
Board	flooded base board 75 mm (3 inch) larger all round than cake
Flowers	5 carnations 5 sprays blossom 10 bunches tiny tims 10 leaves
Ribbons	6 bunches with long tails 2 metres red velvet ribbon

SPECIAL NOTE:
Board edge is finished with red velvet ribbon.

Red-tipped carnations with ribbon loops and trails are set at the rear of this simple cake.

L'AMOUR

An elegant design featuring a single rose and blossom sprays on each tier.

SPECIAL NOTE:
Unusual lace treatment uses tiny cutter flowers in between lace pieces.

You will need:

To Bake	3 hexagonal cakes
Boards	base board 50 mm (2 inch) larger all round than cake middle and top boards 25 mm (1 inch) larger all round than cakes

Flowers
5 small roses
4 large roses
35 blossom

12 bunches

TRAILING ROSES

Beautiful summer roses and wedding bush are used to perfection on this simple cake. Small cutter flowers are featured on the drop loop edge at the base of the cake.

You will need:

To Bake

3 hexagonal cakes

Boards

flooded – large board allow 38 mm (1½ inch) all round tin size

middle board allow 32 mm (1¼ inch)

top board allow 25 mm (1 inch)

Flowers

16 summer roses

4 large sprays of wedding bush

20 medium to small bunches of wedding bush

36 leaves in varying sizes

cutter flowers – 3 were attached to each drop loop.

270 flowers needed for a three tier cake

12 bunches baby's breath

Ribbons

17 bunches of 2 mm (¹⁄₁₆ inch) white satin ribbon

FLEUR

A sweet and simple design for a small wedding. The use of a crystal swan and small bush orchids makes this an easy cake for anyone to decorate.

You will need:

To Bake	1 23 cm (9 inch) heart shaped cake
Boards	1 base board 30 mm (³/₁₆ inch) larger all round than cake
Flowers	30 bush orchids
	18 bush orchid buds
	tiny leaves

The romantic look is achieved with the crystal swan floating on a floral bed.

MELODY OF LOVE

The bell shaped cakes featured in this design are very unusual. The offset top tier enhances the cascade effect in the flowers. The unusual treatment of extension work with ribbon insertion at the base adds a dainty finish to the overall design.

Position of the three pillars used to support the top tier.

You will need:

To Bake	1 large flat bell shaped cake
	1 small flat bell shaped cake
Boards	base board cut 10 cm (4 inch) larger all round than cake
	top board cut 50 mm (2 inch) larger all round than cake
Flowers	40 fairy bells
	6 stephanotis
	12 sprays of daphne
	10 sprays of tiny tims with buds
Ribbons	6 small bunches of loops
	2 metres for insertion work

32

APRICOT LACE

Lovely lace and cornelli work add an interesting touch to this pretty cake featuring tiny carnations and mini orchids. The different placement of the flowers on the bottom tier adds further interest.

You will need:

To Bake	1 – 25 cm (10 inch) square cake
	1 – 15 cm (6 inch) square cake
Boards	1 – 33 cm (13 inch) square
	1 – 20 cm (8 inch) square
Flowers	15 carnations
	14 mini orchids
	20 tiny blossoms
	8 leaves
Ribbons	10 bunches of loops

SUMMER LACE

A single tier cake which is very suitable for a small, sophisticated wedding. The dainty lace edge gives a delicate touch.

Lace border

You will need:

To bake	1 – 20 cm (9 inch) square cake
Board	base board 30 mm (1½ inch) larger round than cake
Flowers	6 frangipani
	12 small roses
	5 blossoms
	6 buds
	4 leaves
Ribbons	2 metres double-edged for around the cake
	4 large bunches
	3 small bunches

PROMISE ME

An interesting arrangement for a three tier cake. A specially made perspex stand creates the illusion that the tiers are suspended in the air.

You will need:

To Bake	3 octagonal cakes
Boards	base board 50 mm (2 inch) larger all round than cake
	middle board 25 mm (1 inch) larger all round than cake
	top board 25 mm (1 inch) larger all round than cake
Flowers	15 formal roses
	25 sprays daphne
	20 leaves
Ribbons	20 bunches of loops

DAINTY BELLS

A single tier cake for an elegant wedding. Tiny bells set in among the flowers are a feature to delight any bride.

SPECIAL NOTE:
Lovely edge treatment features cutter flowers in scallops.

You will need:

To Bake	1 oval cake
Board	base 75 mm (3 inch) larger all round than cake
Flowers	15 primulas
	15 violets
	10 baby roses
	12 baby rose buds
	6 bunches bun flowers
	7 petunias
	7 lemon blossom
	14 leaves
	144 cutter flowers
Ribbons	8 small bunches

LUCKY IN LOVE

The horseshoe design is beautifully offset with Australian wildflowers in this interesting design.

You will need:

To Bake   1–25 cm (10 inch) horseshoe shaped cake

Boards   1–35 cm (14 inch) oval

Flowers	1 banksia bloom
	8 sprigs of wattle
	8 flowering gumnuts with buds
	4 gumnuts
	3 sprigs of pink boronia
	2 sprigs of yellow boronia
	4 sprigs of brown boronia
Ribbons	3 bunches of loops with long tails

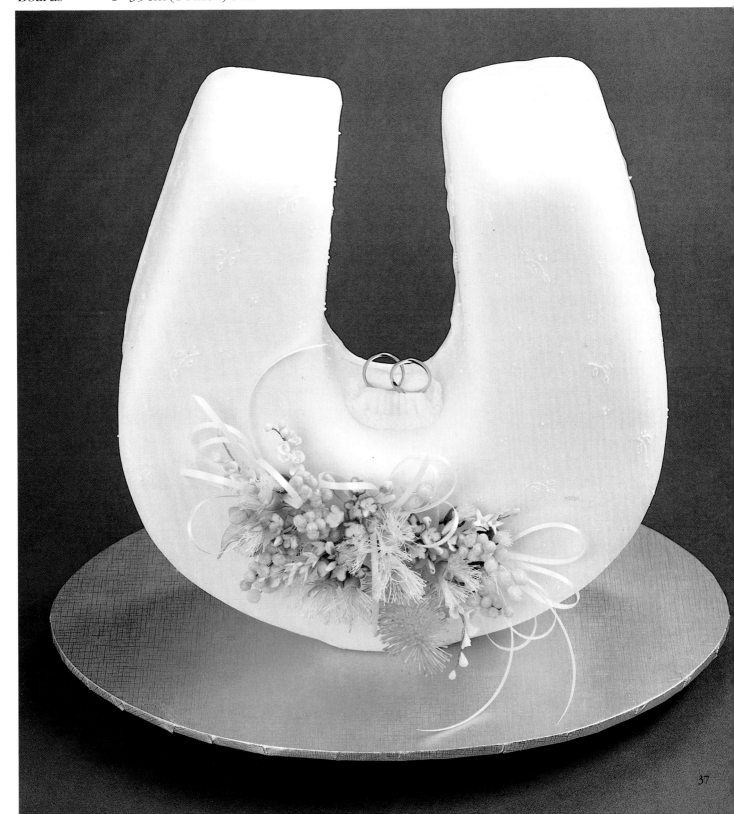

SWEET AND PRETTY

Roses, primulas and jasmine have been arranged in attractive sprays on this sweet and pretty cake. The built out extension is piped on the bell and bottom tier only. Lovely in any colour shades.

You will need:

To Bake	1 – 25 cm (10 inch) round cake
	1 – 18 cm (7 inch) round cake
	1 small bell shaped cake
Boards	1 – 33 cm (13 inch) round base board
	1 – 18 cm (7 inch) round board for middle tier
	1 – 17 cm (6½ inch) round board
Flowers	1 large formal rose
	4 medium formal roses
	20 rose buds
	12 blossoms
	24 primula
	12 sprays pulled jasmine
	20 leaves varying sizes
Ribbons	4 bunches with long tails (for bell top)
	3 large bunches (middle tier)
	2 medium bunches with long tails (bottom tier)

SPECIAL NOTE:
Single pillar has extra wide base top and bottom.

JOY

A miniature bride and groom are set amongst the dainty arrangement of spring flowers. The delicate shading was achieved by covering the cake with white icing, then spraying the sides lemon (deepening the colour towards the board) before painting the embroidery a soft shade of green.

You will need:

To Bake	1 large oval cake
Boards	base board 50 mm (2 inch) larger all round than cake
Flowers	34 spring primulas 12 buttercups 12 bunches fill-in spring flowers 11 small leaves
Ribbons	9 bunches of loops

ALL OUR DREAMS

A church window surrounded by daisies makes this design appealing in its simplicity. Daisies and piped stems make an attractive edge.

Detail showing the construction of the church window.

You will need:

To Bake	1 – 35 cm (14 inch) rectangular cake
	1 – 20 cm (8 inch) rectangular cake
Boards	base board 50 mm (2 inch) larger all round than large cake
	top board same size as cake
Flowers	57 daisies
	10 leaves
	8 sprays of small flowers
Ribbons	6 small bunches of loops

FIRST LOVE

A pretty design for the young at heart. The Victorian posy on the top tier adds a lovely touch to this sweet cake, which features roses and violets.

You will need:

To Bake	1 – 25 cm (10 inch) round cake
	1 – 15 cm (6 inch) round cake
Boards	1 – 33 cm (13 inch) round
	1 – 20 cm (8 inch) round
Flowers	1 large rose
	8 small roses
	6 rose buds
	10 sprays violets
	10 small flowers
	6 leaves
Ribbons	3 bunches with long tails
	4 bunches with small loops

WEDDING BELLS

A lovely idea for the use of wedding bells. The side design has been kept simple so that it does not detract from the small, dainty alpine primula cascade to the tier below, then onto the board.

You will need:

To Bake	1 – 25 cm (10 inch) round cake
	1 – 20 cm (8 inch) round cake
Boards	1 – 33 cm (13 inch) round
	1 – 25 cm (10 inch) round
Flowers	72 Alpine primulas
	24 saxifragas
	12 leaves
	3 small bells
Ribbons	
	15 small bunches
	1 large bow for bell top

AUTUMN HAZE

Autumn tones were used in this interesting arrangement of an oval bottom with a round top. The use of the strong colours is offset by the soft side design.

You will need:

To Bake	1 large oval cake 1–13 cm (5 inch) round cake
Boards	oval base 75 mm (3 inch) larger all round than oval cake 17 cm (7 inch) round board
Flowers	10 double dog roses 28 ivy leaves 33 small blossom flowers
Ribbons	10 bunches

Fine ribbon loops amongst dog roses complete this design.

PINK PEARL

A different but simple design using a specially cut cake for the crescent top. The crescent shape top tier compliments the floral arrangement on the lower tier for a very pretty effect.

You will need:

To Bake	1 – 25 cm (10 inch) round cake
	1 – 20 cm (8 inch) round cake cut to crescent shape
Boards	1 – 33 cm (13 inch) round board top board same size as crescent
Flowers	3 open roses
	5 bunches pulled jasmine
	8 pulled violets
	10 leaves
Ribbons	9 bunches

SPECIAL NOTE:
Top cake is specially cut to crescent shape of a size to compliment bottom tier.

Cut out.

PINK ELEGANCE

An unusual cake using open roses and wedding bush as the feature flowers. The lace medallions add an interesting finish to the lower edge.

You will need:

To Bake	1 – 28 cm (11 inch) round cake
	1 – 20 cm (8 inch) round cake
	1 – 15 cm (6 inch) round cake
Boards	top tier allow 25 mm (1 inch) all round cake
	middle tier allow 25 mm (1 inch) all round cake
	bottom tier allow 35 mm (1½ inch) all round cake
Flowers	9 open roses
	14 sprays of wedding bush
	15 violets
Ribbons	18 bunches
	3 metres for edging

These are the actual sizes of cutters used for medallions.

WISHING

A two tier beauty, with a wishing well to make your dreams come true, featuring a different placement of the tiers.

You will need:

To Bake	1 large oval cake
	1 small oval cake
Boards	base board 50 mm (2 inch) larger all round than large cake
	top board same size as small cake
Flowers	27 baby blue eyes
	16 bunches tiny sweets
	17 ivy leaves
Ribbons	22 small bunches

A tiny wishing well with a swinging bucket sits atop a floral bouquet.

APRIL LOVE

The bridesmaids' colour is introduced into the side design of this cake and to finish the edge of the boards, as well as in the beautiful floral arrangement of April roses.

You will need:

To Bake	1 large hexagonal cake
	1 small hexagonal cake
Boards	base board 38 mm (1½ inch) larger all round than large cake
	top board 25 mm (1 inch) larger all round than small cake
Flowers	2 large open roses
	7 medium roses
	9 rose buds
	31 snow-in-the-summer blossoms
	16 saxifraga
	16 leaves
Ribbons	11 bunches of loops

CHARMING CASCADE

This attractive cake has the top tier offset to the back to allow the dainty flowers to fall in a cascade effect. The bible is set among the flowers and features the names of the bride and groom and a tiny half bell.

You will need:

To Bake	1 – 25 cm (10 inch) square cake
	1 – 15 cm (6 inch) square cake
Boards	1 – 33 cm (13 inch) square
	1 – 20 cm (8 inch) square
	Both boards are flooded with royal icing and finished with gold banding
Flowers	70 Alpine primula
	35 star flowers
	25 leaves
Ribbons	16 bunches of loops

SPECIAL NOTE:
Small amount of tulle to place behind bible.

BLUE LACE

This is an easy style for anyone to attempt. Featuring silk flowers and edge, it can be decorated to suit the colour scheme of your special day.

You will need:

To Bake	1 long oval cake
Board	base board 50 mm (2 inch) larger all round than cake
Flowers	15 silk daisies
	baby's breath
Ribbons	2 metres of silk lace

A three tier design also using silk flowers and ribbon trails.

JUST PERFECT

A very pretty design for the modern bride. Masses of ribbon and flowers add interest and the perspex pillar and ring case give a delicate finish.

SPECIAL NOTE:
Boards are covered in material to match the colour of the bridesmaids' dresses.

You will need:

To Bake	1 large eight blossom cake
	1 small eight blossom cake
Boards	base board 50 mm (2 inch) larger all round than cake
	top board 25 mm (1 inch) larger all round than cake
Flowers	30 kurume azaleas
	25 rose buds
	35 ivy leaves
	20 small sprays of flowers
Ribbons	68 bunches of loops

BOUQUET OF HAPPINESS

A modern treatment for a three tier cake. Lowering the pillars makes the cascade of blossoms flow from one tier to the next. The hanging bells set among the flowers are a special feature.

You will need:

To Bake	3 oval cakes of varying sizes
Boards	base board 50 mm (2 inch) larger all round than large cake
	middle board 25 mm (1 inch) larger all round than medium cake
	top board 25 mm (1 inch) larger all round than small cake
Flowers	80 mountain primulas
	30 small jasmine
	30 leaves
Ribbons	15 bunches of loops large bow of curling ribbon for top of bell pole

SPECIAL NOTE:
All boards are flooded with royal icing and finished with silver banding.

SO IN LOVE

This simple but delightfully decorated cake has a real air of romance. The frilled flounce is caught up with tiny rosebuds.

You will need:

To Bake	1 – 28 cm (11 inch) round cake
	1 – 20 cm (8 inch) round cake
	1 – 15 cm (6 inch) round cake
Boards	1 – 35 cm (14 inch) round
	1 – 25 cm (10 inch) round
	1 – 20 cm (8 inch) round
Flowers	4 large roses
	11 kurume azaleas
	18 baby roses
	41 rosebuds
	18 sprigs of small flowers
Ribbons	5 bunches of loops

TODAY, TOMORROW, ALWAYS

A fresh flower posy is featured in this royal icing fantasy. Arranged around a central pillar the unusual shaped cakes feature piped flowers and leaves with tiny moulded bells. The posy has rosebuds, frangipani, tuber roses with gypsophila, tiny leaves and long ribbon trails.

Two half bells on each cake complete this royal icing fantasy.

You will need:

To Bake	3 corner cut diamond shaped cakes
Boards	each 40 mm (1½ inch) larger all round than the cakes
Flowers	all flowers and leaves are piped in royal icing 120 forget-me-nots 132 buds 180 leaves
Ribbons	included in the fresh floral bouquet

SPECIAL NOTE:

All cakes were given four coats of royal icing to achieve the smooth effect. The stand was specially made to hold the fresh flower bouquet.

Cutting line for the three cakes

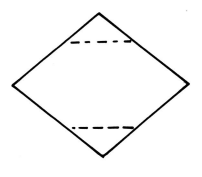

CINDERELLA

An arrangement with a difference for the heart shaped cake. A mass of spring flowes make up the beautiful floral decoration. The handcrafted glass carriage adds a romantic touch to this special wedding cake.

You will need:

To Bake	1–25 cm (10 inch) heart shaped cake
	1–15 cm (6 inch) heart shaped cake
Boards	base board 10 cm (4 inch) larger all round than cake
	small board 50 mm (2 inch) larger all round than small cake
Flowers	20 field daisies
	7 rock violets
	9 roses
	30 wild primulas
	10 blossoms
	14 leaves
Ribbons	
	20 bunches of loops

ROMANCE

This single tier cake would be suitable for a small wedding. This cake is covered in the traditional royal icing method featuring a separate collar with royal icing figures.

SPECIAL NOTE:
Board is flooded in scallops of royal icing to match royal icing collar.

You will need:

To Bake	1 oval cake
Board	base board 5 cm (2 inch) larger all round than cake
Flowers	10 medium cutter flowers
	18 small cutter flowers
	30 tiny piped leaves
	small amount of fine tulle
Ribbons	3 metres

BE MY LOVE

A truly romantic creation featuring red sims carnations and gypsophila. The delicate edge compliments the flower arrangement.

You will need:

To Bake	3 octagonal cakes
Boards	base board 75 mm (3 inch) larger all round than cake
	middle board 50 mm (2 inch) larger all round than cake
	top board 50 mm (2 inch) larger all round than cake
Flowers	14 sims carnations
	20 sprays gypsophila
	30 leaves
Ribbons	16 bunches in varying sizes

FANTASIA

A wedding cake with a difference. The fan shape makes this design very special for the smaller wedding.

SPECIAL NOTE:

Lower edge of the cake is finished with a wide band of satin ribbon cut to scallop shape which was attached after the cake was sprayed to match the colour of the bridesmaids' dresses.

You will need:

To Bake	1 medium fan shaped cake
Board	base board same size as cake
Flowers	9 Singapore orchids
	4 sprigs of maidenhair fern
Ribbons	10 bunches of loops with tails

RHAPSODY IN PINK

Sweet peas together with baby roses and sprays of sweet rocket have been arranged in an unusual way on this impressive two tier cake.

SPECIAL NOTE:
Hand-moulded bell has been back blushed and baby roses threaded through the florist's bow. All boards are flooded with royal icing.

You will need:

To Bake	1 – 25 cm (10 inch) square cake
	1 – 15 cm (6 inch) square cake
Boards	1 – 32 cm (13 inch) square board
	1 – 20 cm (8 inch) square board
Flowers	17 sweet peas
	49 baby roses
	29 sprays of sweet rocket
Ribbons	22 bunches of loops